A Few Poems for *Alice*

HENRY H. GRAY

*To my good friend
Betty —
Enjoy the foolishness —
Henry*

authorHOUSE

Untitled, Unfinished

Was it her hair, her eyes, her smile—
    No, none of these alone,
But something from within her shone
    And captivated me.

Though now a lifetime's passed,
    Still hand-in-hand we walk
. . . . .

Trailside Reverie

Pause—and take in the silences,
    Silences that surround you,
Silences that arrive unannounced,
    Silences that are hard to find,
Silences of eternity—
    While all around you life springs ever anew.

Arctic Circle

we waited
and we waited
as the Sun slipped ever farther north
threading endless rows of slender Arctic firs
that lined the far horizon, but all our waiting was to no avail
because that night the Sun
never
set

Cats

The cat
Sat on the mat
And that
Is all there is
To say
About
The cat.

And Dogs

The trouble with the dog is that
You cannot make it rhyme with cat,
Or fat, or hat, or sat, or mat,
Or bureaucrat, or technocrat,
Or even Secretariat.
The trouble with the dog is that
You cannot make it rhyme with cat!

Through the Seasons

December's dark and gloomy days
May make us feel quite sad

And January's winds and snows
Make roads and sidewalks bad

In February, sugaring
Brings thoughts that Spring might come

But March's ever-roaring winds
Send thoughts of Spring back home.

Then in April comes the time
When hordes of flowers rally

And May, yes May, that welcome month,
The one we wish would dally.

June brings the solstice when
The sun again turns 'round

And July can be the month when
Celebrations resound

Then in August we may go
To visit some relations

And September may mean back to school,
The end of our vacations

October with its falling leaves
Reminds of Earth's life's trend

November's lengthening shadows then
Portends the year's near end.

Whippoorwill

Whippoorwill! Whippoorwill! Whippoorwill!
The bird's song echoed from deep in the hollow.
"Time for bed!" the boy said. "The whippoorwill says
"Go to sleep! Go to sleep! Go to sleep!"

Whippoorwill! Whippoorwill! Whippoorwill!
"Oh, that incessant bird!" thought the mother.
"All night long he keeps endlessly saying
"Stay awake! Stay awake! Stay awake!"

Whippoorwill! Whippoorwill! Whippoorwill!
All night long, deep in the hollow,
The bird sings over and over, confidently,
"This is mine! This is mine! This is mine!"

Wood Thrush

The notes of a wood thrush,
Liquid silver in the silent woods,
Become diamonds
In the rain.

Midnight musings

I thought I heard a herd of words—
I thought I whirled a whirlybird—
Whirlybird, herd of words,
Herd of birds, whirly words—
    You see my problem!

I thought I saw a sea of saws—
Or did I see a sea of c's?
I seized a saw to saw the seas
But all I saw were a's and b's—
    Now that's a problem!

I dreamt I peeled a pair of pears—
That pair of pears had no appeal—
A peeling pair, appalling pears,
To pare the pair, prepare the pears.
    That ends that problem!

I towed a toad along a road—
But as I towed, the toed toad crowed—
The corn was rowed, the cattle lowed,
I owed an ode to that toed toad—
    He's such a problem!

(continued)

I sought to sue a Sioux named Sue.
It then ensued Sue'd not a sou—
I've come to rue I sued that Sioux.
I'd send Sue soon a billet-doux—
    She is a problem!

I picked a Pict to pack a peck.
The Pict was piqued but said he'd pick.
The piqued Pict peeked down from a peak,
Then quit his peak, but kept his pique.
    Now he's a problem!

If you can see, agree with me—
Or fail to see, then disagree—
Or disagree to see with me
Or not to see, oh, dearie me—
    You see my problem?

Suburban Subliminal (1963)
(hora staccato)

Coffee and curlers and dinner at six
Don't forget butter I told you to stop
Going and coming and coming and going
Down to the village forever you say
Once upon everything Peyton Place also
Now he has left her some cabbage for lunch
Launching pad swimming pool sinus martini
Hair's getting gray dear that's too much to pay
See what she's wearing now drive to the church
Time after time in the hospital died
Billy the nursery school doctor's appointment
Talk about loaded and now PTA
Barbeque pork chops the Wilson's new car
Give it back Tommy just give it back now!
Tell me some more in the garden for cocktails
Wall to wall darling and how was your day?

ANIMAL FARE

The Gwoophlet

The Gwoophlet helps to tend the sheep.
    It does this every day,
But just because it will not sleep
    And cannot run away.

The Hwylymn

The Hwylymn, at the end of day
    Around the campfire subtly lay.
And if you sweetly ask me why,
    I'll answer that he could not lie.

The Bum Biddybump

The bum Biddybump sits at the head of the stair
    And tries to pretend that she just isn't there.
But try though she may, she cannot seem to see
    That she's very apparent to you and to me.

(continued)

The Frittered Fritillary

The frittered fritillary
      Flits most flittery
And looks askance
      At my efforts littery.

The yttll

The yttll sleeps 'til half past one
      And then it takes a nap—
The yttll's life is lots of fun
      If it can find a lap.

What du the kudu du?

The emu doesn't mu
      And the tapir doesn't pir.
What the kudu doesn't du
      I really can't be sure.

(continued)

The Gnu

Is that a gnu—
      Or even tgwu?
Just see them sgnooze!
      I do love gnus.

Tewe chewes tewe ewes

Once on a time there were tewe ewes.
      I scarcely knewe which one tewe chewes.
But rather than request ewer vewes
      I think I'll just go back to gnewes.

Knough-Hough

(Six stanzas in search of an orthodox orthography)

Hough, nough broughn cough!
Wilt though allough
The sough
Behind the plough
To bough?

Once I knough a gal named Sough.
    I dated her a time or tough.
She was a loughlough, through and through,
    But then one day away she flough!

I hough and pough when things get rough
    I'm even grough
      (And sometimes blough)
Yet seldom say "Lay off, McDough!
    "Enough!"

And sough, although I wish to gough
    (To Koughkoughmough)
Both friend and fough
And alsough Jough,
    (Who lives belough)
Must knough.

Oughten sighed he, soughtly coughing,
    Sighed beside my oughfice door,
Looking ough into the oughing,
    Oughful sigh, and nothing more.

At last, it's trough, I come tough yough
    Tough say this howdy-dough
      Is through.
(But in each stanza
    There's a clough!)
      Adough!

Faded Flickers

This is a song of the silver screen
    And of some of the shadows upon it.
Most of these heroes you never have seen
    And never will—doggone it!

Superbly well bred was Sir Hammond Cheese.
    His was a glorious chariot!
As he swung through roles such as "Prince of the Trees,"
    And sinister Judas Iscariot.

"*Mon dieu*" and "*En garde*," it's Etienne Bouillabaisse,
    He of the courtly carriage!
Lover supreme to the end of his days,
    And master of multiple marriage.

Short in the saddle sat "Two-gun" Magee,
    Yet in horse operas he was a classic.
Until one grim day, when intending to flee,
    He met up with an arrow, thoracic.

And we can't overlook Lady Hevilley-Wydde.
    Oh, you think she's not a hero?
Played to the hilt every role that she tried,
    Excepting for one—that of Nero.

This is a song of a past long gone
    And of heroes who made not a riffle.
If you missed them before, you won't miss them for long,
    For you know they were not worth a piffle.

More Animals

The Quid

There is not always *quid pro quo*
Though *ipso facto* it might seem so.
Yet every *quo* must have its *quid*
As every *ego* has its *id*.

The Squid

Consider now the lowly squid
Whose *ego* is below his *id*.
For you to see that lowly squid go
Just denigrate its *superego*.

The Lion

The lion feasts on wildebeest
Not knowing it's a gnu.
I'd think he'd find another kind
To dine on, wouldn't you?

(continued)

The Apostrophe

Its never placed right, the apostrophe,
Nor is it's friend, the only.
If only Im the one to see
This, believe me, its quite lonely.

Pretty Kitty

Kitty, kitty, itty bitty
Oh so cute and oh so pretty.
Can you tell me why it is that
Kitty must become—a cat?

Pills
Pills
Pills!

Pills to the right of me
Pills to the left of me
Pills all around me
Rattled and spilled!

Pills before breakfast,
Pills after lunch
I don't know how many!
They sure are a bunch.

Big pills, small pills,
Short pills, tall pills,
Any kind at all pills,
Pills, pills, pills!

Pills of all colors,
Red, white, and blue.
Any kind of color
And bicolor too.

Pills here, pills there,
Pills, pills, everywhere,
Capsules, tablets,
Gelcaps, caplets,

Pills
Pills
Pills!

Modern Poetry?

Is it
The music of the words
Or is it
The music of the spheres?

It is not
Altogether unincomprehensible
And yet
What is there?

Is there a there there,
Or is there no there there?
Who knows?
Not I!

Batter Up

Betty, better beat the batter.
      Butter batter must be beaten
            Or the batter becomes bitter.
                  Bitter batter can't be eaten.
Betty, better bring the beater!
Beat the butter batter better!

Ode to a capsule

Oh, thou capsule of dark mystery,
What may there be inside thee,
And why may I not subdivide thee?
Holy must thou be
As wholly must I swallow thee.

Some deeper thoughts—

The Mustard Seed

What is God? I can more clearly tell you
What He is not
Than what He is.

>God is not a rainbow
>Nor a flower blooming
>Nor even a lightning bolt.

These things all lie within the realm
Of human understanding.
Therefore they are not God.

>Nor is God the thought that hides
>Within the innermost recesses
>Of my mind.

That may yet prove to be
Only a patterned molecule
Or a set of electrical impulses.

>Yet there resides a doubt
>A grain
>No bigger than a mustard seed.

>>Can the entire human experience
>>Be but a set of purely
>>Physical sensations?

(continued)

What's the answer to
That troublesome question
Of my unique identity?

Indeed, why may I speculate at all
Upon the existence
Of a god?

Burgeoning knowledge strips away illusion, sham,
And error, with which our race
Has ever clothed our gods.

Even—perhaps especially—the God
That once walked the earth
Like a man.

Knowledge has come far
But the distance is finite;
Ignorance, on the other hand, is limitless.

Beyond the clangorous Known,
Beyond the whispers of the Knowable,
Beyond the darkness of the Unknown,

Beyond the farthest limit of the empty Unknowable,
Beyond anything comprehensible
Through man's senses and experience

There will always be the ultimate mystery,
In the emptiness of which
Is,
    Or may be,
        Or perhaps once was,
            God.

Communication?

Scarcely more than a hundred years ago
      A man named Marconi
Sent a brief message through the ether,
      Across an ocean.
Today, and every day, and all day, that same ether
      Carries uncountable messages,
In numberless languages, from countless devices
      To countless other devices,
Person-to-person or widely broadcast
      Across every ocean, around the Earth,
And even into space. And I wonder—
      Is anyone listening, or are we all
Shouting in the wilderness?

Reflections

Drop
A pebble
Into a quiet pool.
Watch the ripples spread
Out and out until at last, reflecting
On the distant shore
They slowly
Die.

Drop that same pebble
Into troubled waters of another generation. The ripples won't be so apparent but they'll be there just the same.

A Short History of the Human Race

The history of the human race
can be summed up very briefly:

Men gather in groups
and think up excuses
for making war
on other groups
while women and children
stay home and weep.

And whereas once chieftains
led their followers into battle,
with the coming of
what is called civilization
chieftains remain
in secure locations
and send other peoples' children
to fight their battles.

Extinction

When the last human being
> Puts out the last light

And the darkness of ignorance
> Settles again upon the Earth

The really important questions
> Will yet be unanswered—or unasked—

Voyage's End

I hear the surf upon the distant shore.
      What 'waits me there,
A gentle beach or jagged rocks,
      And what beyond?
I hear the surf upon the nearing shore,
      And only when I get there will I know.

Edwards Brothers Malloy
Oxnard, CA USA
September 9, 2013